THE INKER'S SHADOW

ALLEN SAY

SCHOLASTIC PRESS · NEW YORK

IN MEMORY OF MRS. LAURA SWOPE AND MR. NELSON PRICE

Library of Congress Cataloging-in-Publication Data available

ISBN 978-0-545-43776-9

10 9 8 7 6 5 4 3 2 1   15 16 17 18 19
Printed in Malaysia 108
First edition, October 2015

The art for this book was created using watercolors, pen and ink, pencils, and photographs. Text was set in 13-point Monotype Fornier. Captions were set in a font based on Allen Say's handwriting. Book design by David Saylor and Charles Kreloff

Noro Shinpei cartoons that appear on pages 3 and 17 are reprinted by permission of Kunio Takama, executor of the estate of Noro Shinpei. All photographs courtesy of the author.

WHEN I WAS A SMALL BOY IN JAPAN, I wanted to be a cartoonist.

At twelve, I became a student of a famous cartoonist named Noro Shinpei. I called him Sensei, which means "teacher" or "master."

The master gave me a new name, Kyusuke, and put me in one of his comic book serials.

At first Kyusuke was my cartoon double. But soon he became famous while I was still a middle-school student. I inked a lot of the world he ran around in and thought of him as my comic shadow. It bothered me sometimes that his fans knew nothing about me.

Kyusuke traveled the world with only a knapsack on his back. Wherever he went, he got in trouble, but trouble was adventure for him. I was jealous of his freedom.

I was fifteen when I decided to go to America and make a name for myself.
Instead of a knapsack, I traveled with a cardboard suitcase and a paint box
that Sensei had given me. I was determined to become a cartoon artist.

In the summer of 1953, I came to America with my father and his new wife and their baby girl. We landed in Long Beach, California. Father's American friend, Bill, met us at the dock.

"Don't disgrace me in America," Father said to me in front of the house Bill had rented for them. He gave me ten dollars as I said good-bye.

Then Bill drove me to a town called Glendora.

"You son of a gun!" Bill exclaimed.

He had called me that when I was small, until I thought maybe that was my name in English. Now he kept talking as he drove, and I recognized a few words now and then. He asked about my mother.

"Thank you, fine," I said. He gave me a squeeze on my shoulder.

The town of Glendora was like an Edward Hopper painting with palm trees. The main street was three or four blocks long, sunny and empty. There were no traffic lights. Bill had been homesick for this place when I knew him. What would he think of Tokyo now, I wondered.

The last time I had seen Bill he was driving a jeep in Sasebo, the harbor town on the south island of Japan. The war had just ended. I was eight. He was an officer in the American Occupation Force.

Somehow, Bill and my father became good friends. He visited us often, bringing gifts of things we hadn't seen in years—sugar and butter for our parents, chocolates and chewing gum for me and my sister. He was like a Santa Claus in a jeep.

Best of all, he gave me American comic books. They were the first cartoons I had ever seen in color. I pored over them until they fell apart.

We knew Bill for about a year before he went back to California. He and my father kept up their friendship by mail.

Now, seven years later, Bill drove me to his house on the campus
of the school that his father had founded before the war. It was called
Harding Military Academy. My father had paid my way to America
for me to attend it. Bill was my sponsor. I was to work for my tuition.

Bill introduced me to his family. His wife, Peggy, spoke to me slowly in the way she spoke to her two children. Her speech was easier to understand than anyone else's.

Bill's mother smiled kindly. His father, Major Harding, said, "Welcome to our great country," and went back to his magazine.

Outside, a crowd of boys surrounded me. "Meet Allen," Bill said.
"Hi, Al!" "Hi, Al!" "Hi, Al!"

They were friendly and very curious about a new arrival from their former enemy country. An old woman called Housemother hovered behind them.

"Let's get you situated,"

Bill said. *Let's – get – you – situated*. I said his words in my head.

Repeat and memorize everything I hear! Ask whatever I don't understand; you're not in Japan anymore, nobody is watching you; go ahead, make a fool of yourself and learn!

Listening and asking, I understood that I came in the middle of a summer camp, that the regular classes will start in September.

But the place didn't look like a school. It was more like a park with bungalows here and there. Bill called them barracks. I put the word in my mental notebook. Barracks: plain houses that kids can draw.

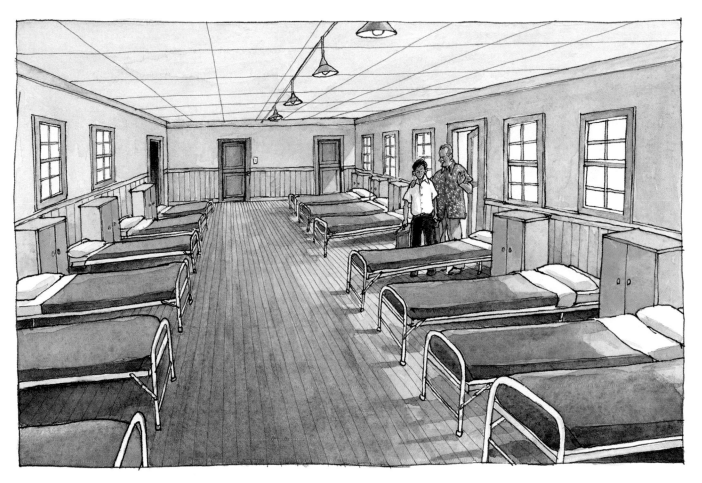

"Welcome to your new home," Bill said.

It looked like an empty hospital or a penitentiary. He pointed at one of the cots and I laid my paint box on it.

Bill opened the doors of the locker by the cot.

"Get squared away and come to dinner."

That was clear. I put my things in the locker and walked down to his house.

At dinner, Peggy explained that the boys in my barracks were away and that I had the place to myself for a few days. The dinner was like the food I'd had on the freighter for two weeks. No rice.

I got back to the barracks early. Or so I thought. But just as I was getting my sketchbook out, a door opened and the housemother poked her head in.

"Good night, Al," she said, and turned out the lights. It was seven-thirty! I hadn't even brushed my teeth.

Is this a joke? Artists don't go to bed at seven-thirty . . . kids don't go to bed at seven-thirty! I haven't drawn anything since I got off the ship. What kind of a place have I come to?

A panic came over me. But the singing crickets calmed me a little—they sounded just like Japanese crickets. Then the singing turned into a voice calling my name. I looked out the window and swallowed a breath.

"Kyusuke!"

"It's me."

"You stowed away!"

"Sensei told me to keep an eye on you . . ."

"You're mad! You couldn't hide in Bill's car!"

"I don't take up much room . . ."

He came in and sat on the next cot.

"What a fun place! All these beds to sleep on!"

"You can't stay here!"

"Why not? You're all tucked in cozy."

"I'm going to work. I'm going to earn my keep here."

"Well, good for you!" He shook off his shoes and flopped down.

"Then take off your stupid hat!"

He was fast asleep.

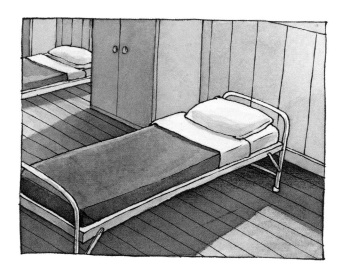

In the morning a loud bugle call woke me. The next cot was neat and empty. I'd only dreamed Kyusuke . . . but I couldn't shake the feeling he was lurking near me and snickering.

The next thing I knew I was out on the playground with a bunch of boys who seemed to have come out of nowhere. I recognized a few of them from yesterday, and I was glad I didn't have to share my barracks with them.

A fellow a couple of years older than me blew his whistle and I did jumping jacks with *gaijin* schoolkids, except I was the *gaijin* now, the foreigner.

Bill introduced me to the staff of the mess hall kitchen. They were Cook Number 1, Cook Number 2, and their helper, named Martha.

"How many pancakes, honey?" Number 1 asked. I knew pancakes, but *honey* was what Bill called his wife.

"Yes, please," I said.

Number 1 gave me a heaping plate, like an offering at some temple. I ate three pancakes and thought about the times I had been hungry. My breakfast would have fed my family for a whole day. Martha dumped what I didn't eat in a garbage can.

"Okay, honey, it's fun time," Martha said.
I wore an apron for the first time.

The kitchen made me think of the comic books Bill had given me—maybe the Katzenjammer Kids, or some other bad boys who had to wash dishes as punishment.

But this was my job, to pay for my education.

Martha was a good teacher. But you don't need a lot of training to wash dishes. I could do it as well as anybody, even if I didn't understand what my bosses said. *I'll be the best dishwasher in America!*

FROM DEMOKURASHEE—CHAN BY NORO SHINPEI, IN MAY 28, 1951, ISSUE OF *SCHOOL CHILDREN'S NEWSPAPER*

Mopping the floor made me think of Kyusuke's job on a foreign ship. He was constantly in trouble with his bosses but always managed to go on to other jobs, taking on anything that came his way.

That's it! Be like Kyusuke! Life's an adventure!

"Step on the tiger's tail," as Sensei would say, "and run like crazy!"

I am Kyusuke!

After the morning mess I helped a handyman named Willard to paint walls and windows. It was more fun than scrubbing pots and pans. *Imagine you're painting murals in one color!*

"You got a good hand, kid," Willard told me.

Then an old man named Hank taught me to run the lawn mower. He was the housemother's husband.

"Always carry a sketchbook and use it," Sensei had told me the first day I became his student. I had obeyed him for four years, until now.

I'm Kyusuke! I'm having a good time!

There are holes to be dug everywhere you go in the world. But I wasn't a kid anymore—I couldn't dig through to the other side of the earth. I was already on the other side!

And holes are to be filled up again. Dig and fill, fill and dig— for education and fame!

But when I thought about drawing, I stopped being Kyusuke. I imagined skiing down a snow-covered mountain and drawing beautiful lines behind me. But it was no good. I had to do it in a sketchbook.

I trained my karate knuckles, to make them as hard as stones . . .

BANG BANG BANG BANG BANG BANG

The boys were practicing for war with real guns and bullets. Guns were called rifles, or weapons, bullets were ammo. I remembered a teacher who said that if you give a boy a knife, sooner or later he will use it. These boys would soon be GIs and shoot in real wars.

That night in the mirror, I turned back into Kyusuke.

"Karate is useless in America," I told him.

"You're supposed to be drawing, not hitting walls," he said.

"Draw what?"

"What's around you . . ."

"We're in a latrine," I said, using a new word I had just learned.

"Start drawing."

"Toilets and showerheads? Very funny."

"You've drawn teakettles and old shoes. What's the difference?"

I didn't have a good answer.

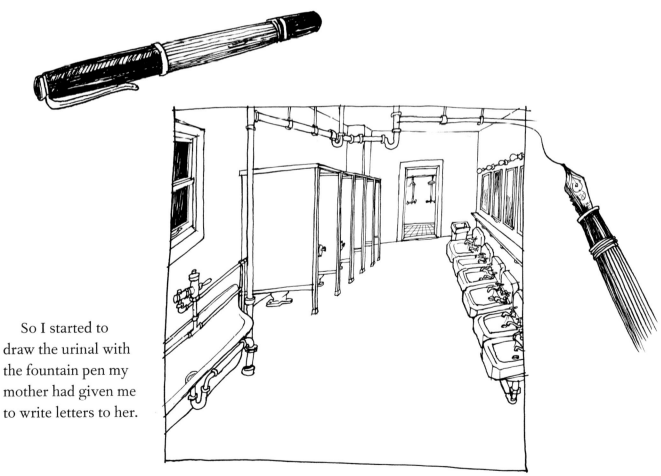

So I started to draw the urinal with the fountain pen my mother had given me to write letters to her.

But everything I drew turned into cartoons.

And Willard caught me at it.

"Come with me," he said.

"This is no art school, kid. The only thing I can teach you in a place like this is driving."

"Drive car?"

"If you want to get around in this country."

"You're looking pleased with yourself," Peggy said.

"Willard teach me drive."

"No, he is not! You need a learner's permit. You are not ready for the test. Come with me!"

She made me read aloud from children's books.

"It's moTHer, not mudder!"

"Look at my mouth! Say MoTHer . . ."

"Muzzar . . ."

"Look me in the eye," Peggy kept telling me. It's rude to do that in Japan.
"I do like men in uniform," she said. I looked like a fake GI and talked like one.

But Peggy wanted me to talk like her. She put me in her sixth grade. Thirteen- and fourteen-year-olds were my upperclassmen. They enjoyed teaching me bad words, and I enjoyed learning them.

"Yes, sir, no, sir, three bags full, sir!"

SOME OF THE TEACHERS

The barracks filled up. The lieutenant liked to surprise his private army.

"Atten-hut!" Freeze!

"Chest out, gut in! Swallow that gum!"

Rex, the cadet sergeant, is caught with a lighter.

"You're busted, Blevins! You're a buck private as of now! And don't let me catch you smoking again!"

"Buck, buck! Private, private, just like us!"

Rex was fourteen and shaved every day. His ambition was to be sixteen, lie about his age, join the Marines, and fight a war.

"I got nothing against you, buddy," he said. "But my pop fought against you guys. He wants to know what you're doing here."

"I don't know," I said. I wished I knew.

Rex called his pop on Monday, and on Wednesday Bill gave him new stripes. Rex had a sewing kit and knew how to use it.

Like his father, Bill was a major now, looking like an older Steve Canyon, the hero in a comic book he gave me when he was only a lieutenant. And I couldn't call him Bill anymore.
    "Yes, sir, no, sir!" Day and night.

The same day Rex got his stripes back, Major Bill said to me, "How would you like to have your own room?"

"I like, sir!" I saluted him.

Above the mess hall was like a small hotel where Willard and Martha had their rooms. There was an empty room up there—a little studio where I could draw at night!

Major Bill led me up to the storage room behind the building.

"Clear out the stuff and you'll have plenty of room. Willard will help you get squared away."

I saluted him again.

"Don't touch those, they're poisonous," Willard said. We killed black widow spiders as we took out bedsprings and dead mattresses.

When my room was set up, I thought about Van Gogh. He would've liked the slanted floor and the kerosene heater. The door on the right led to the toilet and the shower stalls in the hallway.

We made several trips to the town dump. It was incredible what we threw out. In Tokyo, we could have sold most of the stuff to junk shops and made a lot of money.

After the last trip to the dump, Willard handed me the truck key.

"I don't have driver permit," I said.

"We'll fix that." He drove me to the car registration office in the next town, called Azusa. I didn't even have to take a test. In five minutes I walked out with a permit in my wallet.

Teaching me to work the gear stick, Willard must have thought I was stupider than American boys. But he was calm and relaxed even as I kept killing the engine. "Easy does it . . ."

Finally the truck lurched ahead.

Kyusuke in the cartoon world!
"We're getting you on the freeway this weekend, fella." Willard laughed.

Saturday morning, Willard didn't come down for breakfast. The kitchen regulars came and went. No Willard. I asked the cooks.

"He's gone, honey," said Number 1.

"What do you mean?"

"He's not coming back," said Number 2.

"Fired, you mean?"

"You got it. The bottle gets them all. The major won't stand for it."

Martha gave me a sad look.

MY DUCKY!

Sensei was right: To draw is to discover. I discovered that anger is good for cartooning. The angrier I drew, the funnier the drawings turned out.

Did that mean cartoonists are angry people?

MY STICK!

I thought about Sensei. I couldn't remember him ever being angry. But he had been a political cartoonist before I met him, and you *have* to be angry to draw politicians.

The replacement for Willard came in a hot rod. His name was Jack. He had many cars, all with their hoods taken off. He bought "jalopies," he said, and fixed them and sold them cheap. He tried to sell me one; I told him I didn't have a driver's license. So he taught me to drive in his noisy and powerful cars. I started to save money by painting porches and doing yard work for Peggy's church friends.

By the time the school term ended, I'd learned enough English to pass the driving test. Barely.

Around my first anniversary in America, July 1954, Jack showed me a car with its hood still on.

"A '46 Ford. Yours for fifty bucks," he said.

"No radio, busted gas gauge. Just keep her filled up."

I drove it around the campus once and bought it. I had enough money left over for two fillings of gas.

Even Sensei couldn't have imagined Kyusuke driving his own car in America!

YOU BOUGHT WHAT?!

YOU CAN'T DRIVE WITHOUT INSURANCE!

WHAT'S THAT?

Where was the freedom I'd heard so much about? I owned the car "lock, stock, and barrel" as Jack said. It sat in the parking lot like a dead mattress.

"What a beauty! I wish I had a car like this," Martha said.

I promised to give her the first ride when I got my insurance. But that was going to cost twice what I had paid for the car! I did more yard work and painted houses when I should have been drawing. How does anybody become an artist?

And I didn't keep my promise to Martha.

A day after my seventeenth birthday, she disappeared.

"The major wouldn't stand for it," the cooks said.

Gone like Willard, like all the men teachers. Except the little lieutenant who was back already, waiting for his army to arrive.

It was Saturday. I waited until midnight before sneaking out. On the third try the car started. I coasted down the driveway without the headlights.

"It's about time we went somewhere," said Kyusuke.
"So where do you want to go?"
"New York!"
"We've got about thirty dollars, and I have to eat."
"You can always wash dishes, mow grass, paint . . ."

"You know what? I forgot to bring my sketchbook!"
"Sensei will forgive you. Get on the freeway. We're going to see the *real* America!"

"Just think! We can go to Alaska or Argentina!"

"No wonder Americans don't stay in one place."

"Just get on the freedom-road and go anywhere they want."

"But you need a car. Martha doesn't have one. Where could she go? Where is she now?"

"You know what? I don't think Jack put much gas in this car . . ."

"Get off the freedom-road!"

We coasted down a ramp and the car died. A little after four o'clock, nothing would be open now . . . but a train came.

"Are you lost, young man?" a train engineer asked.
"I ran out of gas, sir."
"I can help you with that."
"But you are working . . ."
"Oh, no, I've been retired three years . . ."

"I delivered mail for thirty-eight years but always wanted to work on trains. Now I come out every morning to see this . . ." he said. "And these fellas slow down for me. They're like old friends. So let's get you some gas.

"That switch house came up for sale two years ago. I was very lucky. I'd ask you in, but the missus is still sleeping."

He drove me to a service station where I bought a gallon of gas. He watched me start the car and said, "Come back sometime, I'll tell you all about trains."
I thanked him and got back on the freeway.

"For thirty-eight years that man worked at a job he didn't like," I said.

"He was dreaming."

"He still is—like a boy in a sailor suit."

"Look at that car, it's just like ours."

"One behind us, too."

"Hey, we're lined up with our past and future on the freedom-road, and we can keep going like this for thirty-eight years, like that train man. I have to get off! I should be drawing!"

I turned the car around and got back to a different world. The smog had blown away, baring the mountains I didn't know were there. Everything looked fake, like a postcard.

Sunday afternoon, about three.

At the top of the driveway stood the last person I expected to see: my father. How long had he been waiting there? Through the dirty windshield I could see the thick veins on his head.

He gave me a short speech.

"The Hardings don't think you will make a wholesome American. They are giving you one week to find your own place to live."

I thanked him, asked him to thank the Hardings, and went up to my room.

I came down in fifteen minutes. Father was gone. I felt eyes on me but no one came out, not even a cat or a dog.

My car was dead.

"Major Bill! You used my father to throw me out!"

"He thought your father would take you back."

"Bill doesn't know him. Father is a prince to his friends, but to his family he's an ogre. He abandoned Mother, now it's my turn."

"But he *is* your father, he paid your way . . ."

"What do you know about fathers? You don't have one!"

"I've got Sensci, he's my father!"

How could I forget? I'm Kyusuke! Who needs a father! Good-bye, Father! Good-bye, Major Bill!

But where will I get my dinner? Where will I sleep tonight?

Oh, let me be an old man looking back on today!

There was only one hotel on the main street. It was called Citrus, like so many other businesses in town.

The frayed carpets were stained and smelled of creosote. I could have been in the oldest building in California.

"Yeah," the manager greeted me.

"Do you have a room, sir?"

He looked me up and down. "A buck and a half a night or eight-fifty a week."

"Two weeks, please," I said and gave him the last paper money I had, a twenty-dollar bill.

The smell wasn't so strong in the room, and the floor wasn't tilted to make me dizzy. It was probably bigger than Van Gogh's room, and I had my own washbasin. The toilet and two shower stalls were at the end of the long hallway.

At the store across the street I bought peanut butter and crackers.

On my way out, two policemen stood in my way.

"Hi," I said. I had seen the shorter one shoot his pistol at the academy rifle range. I even changed the targets for him a few times, but now he gave me a cold stare.

"What you got in there?" the taller one asked.

"My dinner, sir."

"Let's see it."

"Put your hands up," he said and shoved me to the wall and frisked me from top to bottom just like in a movie.

"Three bucks in the wallet . . . a quarter, two pennies."

"He's got a receipt, forty-eight cents . . ."

Suddenly the empty street filled with people who had lost their voices. I was in a silent movie. "Kyusuke!" I shouted silently.

HE—HE . . . PLEASE STOP TICKLING AND I SHOW YOU OTHER POSES I CAN DO, SIR!

The policeman's voice woke me. The disappointed crowd scattered. One of them was Mr. Brewer, my new landlord.

He's going to throw me out . . . Will he give me back my money?

I ate my dinner and waited for a knock on the door. It never came.

"He knows you didn't do anything wrong," Kyusuke said.

"So why didn't he tell the policemen I'm his tenant? Nobody will help us here . . . You know, we haven't slept in two days . . ."

Sleep for now, the bed is mine for two weeks.

In the morning I walked to the next town, where nobody would recognize me from yesterday. I had to get a job. A high school and junior college named Citrus stood in the way.

I was going to be in the seventh grade at the academy. No matter how many times I counted, I would be an old man of twenty-two when I finished high school. But first I had to be in school to start serving my time. It seemed like a life sentence. With no hope in my heart, I went into the registration office.

"The fall term doesn't start until next week," a woman said.

"I want to see the principal," I told her. I'd learned Peggy's lesson: Stare back!

She led me to the principal's door and knocked.

"Come in," said a man's voice.

"*Konnichiwa!*" a man greeted me from his desk. I froze.

"I fought against your people; I was stationed in your country. I loved it. Have you ever climbed Mount Fuji?"

"No, sir," I said.

"Well, I climbed it twice!" he said. We laughed together.

It was an old Japanese joke: You are a fool if you don't climb Mount Fuji once in your life; you are a fool if you climb it twice.

We two fools introduced ourselves. He was Mr. Nelson Price, the principal of Citrus Union High School.

"Sit down, son, what's the problem?"

I almost choked. A man I'd never met before called me "son"—a word my father never used for me.

When I mentioned the academy, Mr. Price swore like a
GI. I didn't have to explain very much.

"Write to your old school in Tokyo and have your
transcripts sent to me," he said and gave me his address.
Next he asked if I had a job. No, sir. He spoke on the
telephone for a while, then gave me another address.

"Welcome to Citrus Union, son, you're a junior starting
next Monday. Now go to the address I gave you."

I didn't break down as I thanked him.

But I did outside.

Yesterday I thought I was going to jail or to sleep in an orange grove. Today I leap four years in
my schooling, and maybe have a job! One kind American changed my world.

Even the scabby mountains looked brand-new.

The address Mr. Price gave me was a printing shop in Azusa. The owners, Mr. and Mrs. Mulberry, were waiting for me.

"Mr. Price spoke very highly of you," Mr. Mulberry said.
"We would like for you to work for us," said his wife.
"Yes, ma'am."
"The pay is seventy-five cents an hour."
"Yes, sir!"
"When can you start?"
"Now, sir!"
"Ed will show you what to do."

"So you want to be a printer."
"Yes, sir!"
"Call me Ed."
"Yes, sir, Ed."
"All right, we're going to give this baby a bath."

First the rollers came off. There were many. It was like taking apart a small locomotive that ran on ink. Wipe everything clean with solvent and put it back together. It was a perfect job for Kyusuke.

Running the mimeograph machine was easier than washing dishes. And if you can wash dishes, you can mop floors and clean toilets.

On Friday I received my first pay. I could pay for two weeks' rent, a couple of sketchbooks, a big tube of white paint, and a lot of fifteen-cent hamburgers.

I bought four canvas boards and painted in my room all weekend. The gas stove was perfect for heating cans of spaghetti.

I wrote Mother and gave her my new address.

On Monday morning, I started at Citrus Union High School as a junior.

Mrs. Swope welcomed me to her art class. The girls like grown women made me nervous with their friendly stares. The boys were less interesting. Everybody was painting or making something different.

I felt self-conscious for being a foreigner, and my paint box didn't help. The students watched me as if they'd never seen anyone paint with oils before.

I got up close to the canvas board Mrs. Swope gave me, and the class disappeared. I was alone with my paintbrush. I thought about Van Gogh with his canvas between himself and the world. The canvas shielded him, like a plate of black glass you hold up to see the sun and not be blinded.

The one class I had to attend every day was PE. The boys played flag football.

The flags had nothing to do with the game.

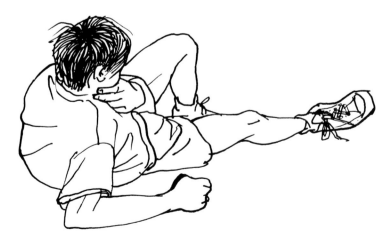

I thought either my jaw or neck was broken. I wasn't anywhere near the ball when the fellow hit me. It took me a while to get up.

I went to the far end of the lineup and the same fellow came over to face me. Veins stood out on each side of his head. I saw in his eyes that he really wanted to break my neck.

No time to run, no time to think. Hut, hut, hike!

He came at me with both arms cocked high; I ducked and struck him in the stomach softer than a punching bag. A gust out of his mouth.

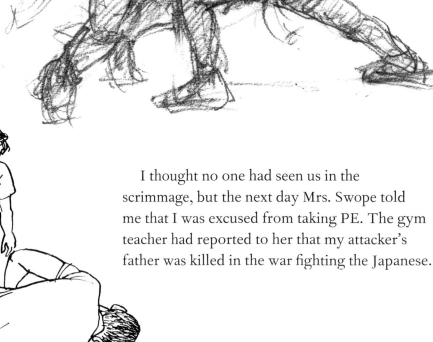

I thought no one had seen us in the scrimmage, but the next day Mrs. Swope told me that I was excused from taking PE. The gym teacher had reported to her that my attacker's father was killed in the war fighting the Japanese.

"Someone who can draw like you should draw fourteen hours a day," Mrs. Swope said. She gave me a Saturday scholarship to an art school called Chouinard Art Institute in Los Angeles.

She introduced me to her other scholarship student, named Bonnie, who knew her way around Los Angeles. I was glad to have her guide me into the big city that Saturday.

The art school was in a building that looked like a factory. But I felt more comfortable there than I did at high school. I was among older students who wanted to be artists.

I'd expected to see a nude model in the life drawing class, but instead a very old nun sat on the platform.

Studying art in factories and convents! No wonder so many American artists had gone to France to learn art. I was in the wrong country!

"Where did you learn to draw?" the instructor asked. His name was Richards Ruben.

"Japan, sir."

"Very French. See me after class."

He introduced me to Mrs. Chouinard, the founder of the school. And there and then she welcomed me, and said that I could take any course I wanted in the following summer.

An instant scholarship! What a great country this is!

Bonnie was very happy for me and took me for a walk in the hills, where she asked me to go dancing with her.

"I don't have a necktie."

"It's not a prom."

"I don't know how to dance."

"It's easy, I'll lead you."

"Don't look at your feet," she said. I looked in her eyes and stepped on her toes. I would never be a dancer, it made me too nervous.

Later I heard Bonnie had a "steady" boyfriend. That confused me but I wasn't disappointed because she had a girlfriend I really liked. I even bought her a milk shake once and had to eat plain bread that night. She never spoke to me again.

I walked around the campus, looking over my shoulder, expecting an ambush. I had an enemy now, and probably there were others. But I also wanted to run into the girl who wouldn't speak to me.

At work, the job I liked best was making deliveries. I drove the owners' new car and took my time cruising in three towns. And one day I ran into the fellow from PE.

I saw him first. He was coming straight at me. Nowhere to hide. As I started to put down the packages he looked up.

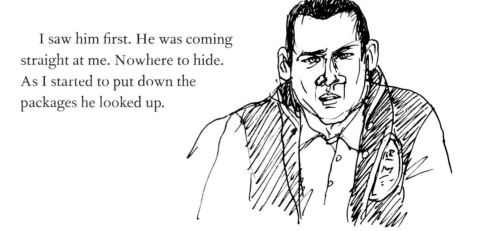

"Hey! How you doing, guy?"
He gave me a big smile.

I almost dropped the packages.
Is this the same fellow?

"Want a hand with those?"

"Oh, no, they're not heavy,
thanks . . ."

"So, where you going?"

I nodded at the door.

"Here you go." He opened it for me!

I almost brushed against him. He could have
smashed my face then, but he just kept smiling. *He
couldn't be the same fellow . . . but then why would a
stranger open a door for me?*

He was gone when I came out.

*Why the turnaround? Was he a Dr. Jekyll
for today?*

"He respects you now . . ." Kyusuke
whispered.

"Because I didn't run like you!"

"But you wanted to . . ."

I swore at him and ran back to the car.

After a few months, Mrs. Swope said, "I can't teach you," and transferred me to the art class in the junior college. It was in a barracks divided into two rooms: one for painting and one for pottery.

Out of the nine or ten students I was the only one who painted with oils. Most of the others worked with clay. The teacher, Mrs. Boseman, knew more about pottery than she did about painting.

A girl named Sylvia wanted to learn printmaking but the college had no equipment for it, so she made charcoal drawings. To save paint, I often drew with her.

LET'S MAKE MONEY!

HOW?

"Draw something Christmassy," she said. "I'll silk-screen it and make some cards to sell."

It sounded like a project for kids, but Sylvia was serious. I agreed to do some drawings and made a date to talk about it.

On Sunday she came in her father's car.

"You live here?" she asked. I nodded.

"By yourself? How neat is that! I'm jealous!"

"Why?"

"You're a free man! You don't have to put up with your parents. How I wish I could be free like you!"

"But this is a free country . . ."

"Not when you have parents like mine. They've been fighting since my sister and I were kids. We beg them to get a divorce but they won't. They hate each other but stay married for us!"

We talked for two hours in the car and became good friends.

The college art room became a kind of private studio for me. And since I didn't have to take PE I went there every day to paint and talk with Sylvia. She brought me sandwiches and loaned me books to improve my English. But before we made any cards she disappeared.

"Sylvia got married," Mrs. Boseman announced to the class.

"Is she coming back?" someone asked.

"She quit school. I think she eloped."

Mrs. Boseman seemed amused.

Why didn't Sylvia tell me?

She was eighteen, a year older than me—a lot of women got married at that age. Maybe she did say something about a boyfriend, but I'd pretended I didn't hear. And now I'd lost my best friend. No one knew where she was.

I should've done some drawings for her . . . then maybe she would've stayed to make cards . . . We could've sold them together . . .

"Why aren't you cartooning?" Kyusuke asked.

"Nothing is funny here."

"Then make fun of the place. You're supposed to be a cartoonist."

"And how do you make fun of orange groves? Art doesn't happen in orange groves . . . and you know why? They're too wholesome!"

"Hmm, I'll have to ask Sensei about that . . ." Kyusuke muttered and faded away into the blinking Christmas lights. Somehow I knew I wasn't going to see him again.

THIS OIL SKETCH ON CARDBOARD IS THE ONLY PIECE OF MY WORK I WAS ABLE TO SAVE FROM THIS PERIOD—MY "BLUE PERIOD," AFTER PICASSO'S.

Three months later, on a spring night, I got back late from work and found a brown bag sitting at my door.

There were two tuna fish sandwiches inside, made with the kind of bread Sylvia liked. I ate one, crying, and saved the other one for breakfast.

Sure enough, Sylvia came to class the next day. She looked older.

So what happened? The marriage was *annulled*, she told the class and gave me a wink.

Later, she explained that *annulment* meant she was never married! It sounded crazy, but I was happy.

"Don't ever get married, Allen, marriage is really stupid," she said. I promised her I never would.

I had a job, a room, a good friend, and I got through my junior year. It was summer again. I could have worked full-time but decided to take the scholarship that Mrs. Chouinard gave me. I went to Los Angeles three times a week, counting my pennies, as Americans say.

I got rides to school from two men who had fought in the Korean War and now were art students. They made me feel like a real artist. I liked them; they weren't wholesome.

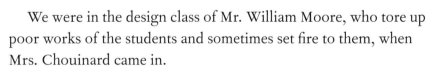

We were in the design class of Mr. William Moore, who tore up poor works of the students and sometimes set fire to them, when Mrs. Chouinard came in.

"Anyone interested in cartooning?" she asked. A famous cartoonist was giving a talk. The students shook their heads; some snickered. I would have raised my hand last year.

At the start of my senior year Mrs. Swope gave me the Saturday scholarship to Los Angeles Art Center School. I was the only one who received it, and that made me feel bad for Bonnie.

The school was in an old mansion, but the inside was even more factorylike than at Chouinard.

There was even a class in designing cars with clay that potters use. And photography—I couldn't imagine anybody spending four years in college to learn to use a camera.

The place felt like a business school. The students looked smug in knowing they would get good jobs after graduation.

None of the courses interested me. I just wanted to paint now, without any business to go with it. Maybe my father was right: I would never be respectable and never amount to anything.

Bonnie was very happy for me for the scholarship and asked me to go to the senior prom with her in May. That confused me. I thought boys were supposed to do the asking, and since the girl I liked wouldn't talk to me, I wasn't going to ask anybody. And what happened to her boyfriend?

But I said yes and was sorry the moment I said it. I didn't have anything to wear for the big dance. I wrote my first "Dear Father" letter asking for a loan of twenty dollars, promising on my life that I would pay him back in one month.

This was his reply:

I regret to note that American high school has been unable to teach you to write proper English.

Father

I read the note three times and went blind. He was his usual self, insulting my high school and calling me an idiot in the same sentence!

I will learn, and one day he will hear about me!

But what to do about the prom costume? A suit, a shirt, a necktie, a pair of shoes. I could wear the old belt and keep the jacket buttoned up and remember not to hike up the pants so the socks wouldn't show . . . then a corsage for Bonnie . . .

It was hopeless. A necktie was about all I could afford, the kind sold in drugstores. I decided to tell Bonnie and lose face forever.

Then I received an envelope from the United States government that had a check in it made out to me for over ninety dollars! I had to show it to Mr. Brewer to make sure it wasn't a mistake.

"It's your tax return, kid," the manager said. I could buy two suits with that, maybe three!

About a month before the senior prom Mrs. Swope took me to a museum in Los Angeles, but when I told her I needed a suit she took me to a department store and chose one for me.

I was frisked the second time. I wanted a darker suit, but Mrs. Swope said that "olive-skinned" people looked better in lighter colors. I listened and bought everything I needed there and still had over twenty dollars left!

I was a boy Cinderella with a mean father! And no fairy godmother could be kinder than Mrs. Swope. And instead of mean stepsisters, I had in Sylvia the older sister I'd always wanted to have. I told her about my new clothes.

"What you want is a monkey suit, Allen," she said. "You know, a *tuxedo*—a dinner jacket with a silly sash like *obi* and striped pants that make you look like a waiter in a fancy hotel . . ."

"But . . ." was all I could say.

"And guess what? Nobody buys any of that stuff—you rent everything!"

It was all about clothes. What to wear for this and that. All *uniforms*! Did I have enough money left to rent a prom uniform? And without a car, how was I to take Bonnie to the dance? I wanted to ask, when she came to me first.

She looked very agitated, almost in tears. She had to cancel our date! Something had come up, she started to explain, but I didn't hear a word of what she said. I had a hard time hiding my relief.

I wore my suit to the graduation ceremony and joined the other suited boys about to become men. The caps and gowns made our uniforms complete, and looking like monks in a procession, we received our diplomas.

When the ceremony ended, I tossed my cap away.
"Here's another funny hat for you, Kyusuke!"

I said good-bye to the people who had been kind to me, and checked out of the room where I had been hungry, not only for food.

I would always be grateful to Mr. Price, and Mrs. Swope, and miss Sylvia very much. But I would not be homesick for anything else.

I will never come back.

Wearing my suit, and my diploma in the suitcase, I got on a bus to San Francisco, the city where my mother was born—the place that she had longed to return all her life.

AUTHOR'S NOTE

Everything is true while nothing is accurate.
— *Georges Simenon*

We remember our past in episodes. We store
them in the bag of memories we call our mind.
There, the passing of time shuffles them,
making some grow larger while stunting
others, and blows many away like smoke.

For this book I picked out some of the
episodes that are still floating in my head and
arranged them into a story about my first
three years in America. It's a patchwork of
memories, and memories are unreliable, so I
am calling this a work of fiction made of real
people and places I knew.

Both of my parents were fluent in English,
but I didn't learn it from them. It was the
enemy's language in wartime Japan, making
it a crime to speak it even in the privacy of a
home. After the war, my parents divorced, and
I didn't begin to study English until I was in a
middle school in Tokyo. By the time I came to
America in 1953 I could read simple children's
books but couldn't carry on a conversation
with preschool kids.

Glendora, the town where I went to school,
sits twenty-two miles east of Los Angeles.
At the time of my arrival it was surrounded
by orange groves and had a population of
five thousand and one movie house. And
there I began my new life as a sixth grader
in a military academy for young boys. I was
sixteen. In three months I could carry on
broken conversations with the boys, who didn't
believe there were trains in Japan. A year later

AT KNOTT'S BERRY FARM, MY FIRST VISIT TO AN AMERICAN
AMUSEMENT PARK, AUGUST 1953

AS A CADET PRIVATE, WITH SHOOTING MEDALS,
OCTOBER 1953

LOOKING FOR AMERICA IN A '46 FORD I BOUGHT FOR $50, AUGUST 1954

MRS. SWOPE TAKES ME SHOPPING IN LOS ANGELES, APRIL 1956

MR. NELSON PRICE IN THE 1956 CITRUS HIGH SCHOOL YEARBOOK, WHICH WAS DEDICATED TO HIM

I talked myself into the local high school.

While attending Citrus Union High School I lived in a hotel named Citrus. It was empty during the week except for the three permanent residents: Mr. Brewer, the manager; a woman in her fifties who walked in the hallways all day in a muumuu dress; and me. Mr. Brewer turned out to be a friendly man. When I could afford them, I bought a dozen eggs—a week's breakfast—which he let me boil in his kitchen. He claimed to be an uncle of Teresa Brewer, the famous pop singer, and told me that she had promised to come visit him in her limousine; he was still waiting when I left two years later. He never raised my rent, which was $8.50 a week.

My take-home pay was twelve to fifteen dollars a week. Every four or five months my mother sent me a check without my asking, always for thirty dollars, a fortune that turned into more paint than food.

Besides the English classes, schoolwork wasn't difficult, and since I lived alone and didn't have a guardian, I could cut classes without excuse slips. I spent my free time painting and drawing in the junior college art room.

When I began working on this book I checked on the Internet to see what I could find on my old high school and came across an unhoped-for treasure: a facsimile of the 1956 yearbook, *La Palma*, for sale! A few days later it came to me as a gallery of forgotten faces, one of them the eighteen-year-old me smiling back at himself across fifty-five years.

And I was very excited to see that *La Palma* was dedicated to Mr. Nelson Price, the principal who left Citrus High that year to become the principal of a high school in another town—the man who had welcomed me off the street and sent me leaping four years ahead in my schooling.

The yearbook also commemorates the retirement of Mrs. Laura Swope, my art teacher, who had taught at Citrus since 1936. She had wanted to be an artist, she confided once, but didn't have the talent,

and dedicated her life to helping young artists.

We parted after my graduation, each of us going our separate ways. I never saw them again. I take the coincidence of our parting personally, as a closure, the end of a chapter. And the chapter got bigger with *La Palma*. I still wonder what my life would have been without them. Would I be an artist today?

Before I could thank them again, they were gone. I know they would have waved away my thanks and said that they were only doing their job.

A job that changed lives.

ALLEN SAY

MY HIGH SCHOOL GRADUATION PHOTO, JUNE 1956

A SUMMER SCHOLARSHIP STUDENT, JUNE 1955

清井